The Breath Before Bethlehem

A cosmic panorama.
Heaven silent, yet alive.
Angels lining the edge of eternity, wings
Folded, eyes fixed downward.
The universe dim, awaiting command.
A divine stillness hangs
Like suspended light.
Then—from the throne—
A pulse …
A breath …
A whisper of Glory rising like dawn.

The Night Heaven Broke

Its Silence

A Christmas Revelation for a Speaking God

Books by Tim Barker

Anticipating the Return of Christ

At Your Feet

Called Camp 2025

Discovering God in the Secret Places

End Times

God's Revelation and Your Future

It's Not All About Sitting at the Head Table

Mighty Men of Courage from the Bible

My Jesus Journey

My Jesus Journey: Crescendo

My Jesus Journey: Glissando

My Jesus Journey: Rhapsody

Names of God

Open Doors

One. Less. Stone.

Our Privilege of Joy

Reflecting Christ Through the Fruit of the Spirit

The Age of Uncertainty

The Authentic Christian: Revealing Christ through the Fruit of the Spirit

The Call of Ephesians

The Lord with Us

The Twelve: Taking Up the Mantle of Christ

The Vision of Nehemiah: God's Plan for Righteous Living

Truth, Love & Redemption: The Holy Spirit for Today

Unified Church

Your Invitation to Christ

The Night
Heaven
Broke
Its Silence

A Christmas Revelation for a Speaking God

Tim R. Barker, D. Min.

Network Pastor/Superintendent
South Texas Ministry Network

THE NIGHT HEAVEN BROKE ITS SILENCE,
Barker, Tim.

1st ed.

Subtitle: A Christmas Revelation for a Speaking God

Scriptures are taken from the HOLY BIBLE, NEW LIVING TRANSLATION (NLT), Copyright© 1996, 2004, 2007 by Tyndale House Foundation. All rights reserved. Used by permission.

ISBN: 979-8-9924875-7-2

DEDICATION

To my wife, **Jill**—
my constant companion, encourager, and the
steady heart that beats beside mine.

To my daughters and sons-in-law,
**Jordin & Stancle Williams and Abrielle & Nolan
McLaughlin**—
your love, faith, and devotion to Christ inspire me
daily.

And to my grandchildren,
**Braylen, Emory & Landon Williams,
Kingston & London McLaughlin**—
may you never lose the awe and wonder of the
Christmas story.

May the miracle of that holy night remain bright in
your hearts, guiding your steps, shaping your
dreams, and reminding you always that Heaven still
speaks.

With all my love,

Pops

PREFACE

The Night Heaven Broke Its Silence

*A Christmas Revelation for a
Speaking God*

There are moments in Scripture that
demand more than reading—they demand
beholding. They are moments where
Heaven leans over the edge of eternity,
moments where angels stop singing,
moments where creation itself seems to
hold its breath.

The birth of Jesus Christ is one of those
moments.

For four hundred years before Christ's
birth, the world turned, empires rose, kings

conquered, nations trembled—and Heaven seemed to say nothing.

No prophet parted the silence.

No miracle broke the quiet.

No fresh revelation stirred the earth.

But then—when the world least expected it … at a time that looked least spiritual … in a place no one would have chosen …

Heaven inhaled.

Heaven exhaled.

And the universe has never recovered.

This book invites you to step into that holy interruption, to feel the weight of 400 years of longing, and to sense the trembling anticipation of angels.

To walk beside the forgotten shepherds and witness the sky ignite with the first worship service since Malachi's final amen.

This is not simply the story of a baby born in Bethlehem.

This is the story of God breaking the sound barrier between Heaven and Earth.

This is the night Heaven refused to remain quiet.

The night the Word became flesh.

The night Eternity stepped into time.

The night Glory wrapped itself in humanity.

The night God descended—not as a warrior, not as a king, but as a whisper that thundered.

And once Heaven broke its silence, it never stopped speaking.

Table of Contents

INTRODUCTION

A Story We Know, A Power We Still Need.

We know this story.

We've memorized the lines.

We've seen grandparents in bathrobes play shepherds. We've watched children wearing tinsel halos sing "Hark the Herald Angels Sing." We've arranged nativity scenes with ceramic animals that never existed in the text.

We've sung about a star we've never seen and a manger we've never smelled.

The danger of Christmas is not commercialization. It is familiarity.

Familiarity blinds us to majesty. Familiarity dulls our awe. Familiarity reduces the miraculous to the manageable.

We've polished the manger but lost the miracle. We've framed the nativity but misplaced the glory.

We've celebrated the holiday but domesticated the holy.

But this book is an invitation to see it again, as if for the first time.

Because the night Jesus was born was not sentimental. It was not tame. It was not cute.

It was cosmic warfare, wrapped in infant flesh.

It was the moment the God of Genesis 1 stepped into the womb of a teenage girl.

It was the moment eternity chose vulnerability.

It was the moment the Lion of Judah arrived as a Lamb.

It was the night Heaven broke protocol, shattered the silence, crushed centuries of waiting—and demolished Hell's plans forever.

This is not a Christmas story. This is a revelation of divine disruption.

We do not revisit this story to remember what happened. We revisit it because it is still happening.

Heaven is still breaking the silence. God is still intervening. Light is still invading the darkness.

And the God who spoke in Bethlehem still speaks today.

CHAPTER 1

THE SILENCE BEFORE THE SOUND

Four Centuries of Quiet — One Moment of Glory

The Heavy Quiet of Heaven

Before there was a manger,
Before there was swaddling cloth,
Before Mary felt a contraction,
Before Joseph heard the first cry—
    there was silence.

Not the silence of peace.
Not the silence of stillness.
Not the silence after a storm.

This was the silence of longing.
The silence of absence.
The silence of a Heaven that seemed
    unreachable.
The silence of a world waiting for a God
Who had not spoken in centuries.

Four hundred years.

That's longer than the United States has
    existed.
Longer than most empires endure.
Long enough for hope to weaken and
    religion to harden.

There were no prophets to challenge kings.
No visions to stir young men.
No dreams to guide old men.
No fresh revelation to break the drought.

Heaven—once a roaring river of divine
    communication—
Had become a still, unmoving lake.

And Israel lived between two Testaments
    like a desert between two rains.

The Door That Would Not Open

A colossal ancient door, towering and
    immovable.
Ivy creeping up its frame.
Cobwebs hanging like forgotten prayers.
Dust thick as history.
Hands—generations of hands—have
    knocked until their knuckles bled.
But the door does not move.
Not even a creak.

This is Israel's spiritual landscape.

Waiting.
Knocking.
Hoping.
Hurting.
Silent.

A grandfather sits by a dim fire, telling a
    young boy:

"Elijah called fire down from Heaven.
I wasn't alive then … but my grandfather

Was told by *his* grandfather
That it happened."

A mother whispers to her daughter:

"Isaiah prophesied a virgin birth.
One day, Messiah will come.
I have never heard God's voice myself …
But the stories say He used to speak."

A priest, lighting incense in a temple
Where God no longer manifests,
    prays:

"Lord … do You still dwell here?
Will You ever speak again?"

Generations lived on memories of glory,
    but not the experience of it.

They believed in a God who *used* to speak.
A God who *used* to move.
A God who *used* to appear.
A God who might speak again someday—
    but hadn't in their lifetime.

The Revelation Hidden
Inside Silence

Here is the truth that Heaven was
   holding:

God's silence is not God's inactivity.

Heaven's quiet is not Heaven's absence.

When God is silent, He is strategizing.

While Earth heard nothing—

Heaven was moving everything.

While Israel mourned the lack of miracles—

Heaven was assembling the greatest
   miracle in history.

While priests cried out for a word—

Heaven was preparing the Word made
   flesh.

The silence was not a void.
It was a womb.

Inside it, prophecy was aligning—

Nations were shifting.
Timelines were converging.
Mary was being born.
Joseph was being shaped.

Rome was building roads for the Gospel,
    and Heaven was preparing an invasion.

The silence before Bethlehem was like
    the silence before a symphony—
The moment the Conductor raises His
    hand right before
The first note splits the air.

CHAPTER 2

HEAVEN'S STRATEGY ROOM

Where Eternity Plans Its Invasion of Time

A Throne Room Like No Other

Before Bethlehem ever heard a newborn's
  cry,
Before shepherds ever saw the sky ignite,
Before Mary ever wrapped God in a
  blanket—

Heaven was preparing.

Not in a quiet corner.
Not in a back room.
Not in secrecy.

But in the throne room of Almighty God—
The most electrifying, terrifying, awe-
  inspiring chamber in existence.

Let's go there.

Slowly.
Reverently.
Barefoot in our spirits.

The Atmosphere of the Almighty

The throne room is not like anything on
  Earth.

There are no shadows—only gradients of
  glory.
The air does not sit still—
It vibrates with holiness.
Every breath feels like inhaling lightning
  and exhaling worship.

Wings rustle.
Light pulses.
Eternity hums like a supernatural
  heartbeat.

Angels—creatures so magnificent that
Humans fall faint when beholding them—
Cover their faces before His throne.
Not because they are afraid of
    punishment—
But because pure glory is too
    overwhelming to behold.

Around the throne, rivers of light flow
Like water made of glory and sound.

Voices cry:
"Holy, holy, holy is the Lord God
    Almighty…"

Their cry does not echo—
It continues, alive, as if each "holy"
    becomes a living creature.

This room is the command center
For everything that has ever happened
And everything that will ever happen.

This is Heaven's Strategy Room.

The Throne of the Uncreated One

A radiant throne made of living light.
Lightning spiraling upward like celestial
  ribbons.
Millions of angels in concentric circles—
Each circle brighter than the last.
The floor made of transparent fire.
The air shimmering with authority.
At the center:
The Ancient of Days.
Clothed in majesty.
Crowned in eternality.
Breathing galaxies.

The Angelic Council Gathers

The room shifts; the atmosphere changes.
An unspoken command ripples through
  Heaven.

A call goes out—
And the greatest angelic assembly since
  Creation begins.

Archangels take their places.
Principalities bow.
Dominions gather.
Warring angels line the perimeter like
blazing sentinels.

Rumors ripple through the ranks:

"Is this the time?"
"Has the moment finally come?"
"Is the prophecy unfolding?"

Gabriel, the messenger of revelations,
steps forward—his face radiant with
expectancy.

Michael, commander of Heaven's armies,
stands tall—
His armor humming with power.
His sword glowing with celestial fire.

All eyes turn toward the throne.

Heaven is waiting.

Earth is breaking.

Hell is trembling.

Heaven's Report on Earth

Gabriel speaks first.

"Lord … look upon the world.
Darkness spreads like a plague.
Israel groans under oppression.
Rome exalts itself.
The hearts of men grow cold.
False kings arise.
Truth falls in the streets.
Fear reigns.
Hope fades."

Michael steps forward, voice thundering
   like war drums:

"The enemy is growing bold.
His strategies are multiplying.
His influence is spreading.
Demons rejoice.
Empires crumble.
Nations rage.
Your people feel abandoned."

Heaven grows silent.
Not like the 400-year silence on Earth—

But the silence of anticipation …
The silence before a decree …
The silence before God speaks.

And then—

With no panic, no urgency, no anxiety—

The voice that crafted galaxies
Whispers a single sentence that shakes
    eternity:

"It is time."

Heaven erupts.

Waves of glory burst from the throne.
Colors unseen by human eyes splash
    across eternity.
Angels fall to their faces.
Light explodes like Creation all over again.

Gabriel grabs his trumpet—
Ready to sound the command.
Michael draws his sword—
Ready to lead Heaven's armies.
Angels prepare for war—
Shoulders squared.

Wings extended.
Ready for holy combat.

And then—
The Lord raises His hand.

A Divine Interruption

"Put the weapons down."

Lightning halts midair.
Wings freeze.
The galaxies pause.
Even the seraphim—the burning ones—
    stop singing.

Gabriel lowers his trumpet.
Michael's hand slips from the hilt of his
    sword.

Confusion ripples across Heaven.

Weapons down?
In a moment like this?
When the darkness is thickest?
When the oppression is greatest?

Then the Lord speaks again—
Not in thunder,
But in tenderness.

"This battle will not be won with force.
This victory will come through vulnerability."

Heaven leans closer.

God smiles—
The sort of smile only sovereignty can
    wear:

"I am sending ... a Baby."

Shock.
A holy gasp.
A cosmic pause.

A Baby?

Heaven expected a King with armies.
A Judge with fire.
A Warrior with ten-thousand angels.
A Lion with thunder in His roar.

But no—

Heaven's invasion would come
  through infancy.

Fragility.
Soft skin.
Small fingers.
Newborn breath.

The Almighty wrapped in weakness.
The Creator carried by a created womb.
The Infinite wrapped in the finite.
The Lion entering as a Lamb.

Heaven's Shock

Gabriel's trumpet lowered mid-breath.
Michael's sword dimming in his grip.
Legions of angels wide-eyed, glowing with
  awe.
The throne radiating with a tenderness so
  bright
That even the seraphim tremble.
Heaven stunned at the strategy of God's
  Love.

The Greatest Strategy Ever Conceived

God continues:

"I will not conquer humanity by
    overpowering them—
But by out-loving them."

"I will not break their chains
    with violence—
But with vulnerability."

"I will not overwhelm them
    with My size—
I will woo them with
    My nearness."

"I will not crush the serpent
    by storm—
But by a Son."

Heaven begins to understand …

The Messiah will not descend
    with armies—
But be born in obscurity.

Not in a palace—
But in a pasture.

Not announced to kings—
But to shepherds.

Not wrapped in silk—
But in swaddling clothes.

Not placed on a throne—
But in a feeding trough.

This is not weakness—
This is divine warfare disguised
    as humility.

Hell expected Heaven to respond
    with thunder—
But Heaven responded with
    tenderness.

The enemy expected
    a sword—
But Heaven sent a Seed.

Because only a Seed
Can crush a serpent's head.

The Decision That Changed Everything

Then with sovereign certainty God
    declares:

"Prepare the womb."
"Position the shepherds."
"Ready the sky."
"Awaken the angels."
"The Word is about to become flesh."

Heaven erupts again—
Not in confusion,
But in worship.

Because the plan is perfect.

The strategy is flawless.

The invasion is unstoppable.

The silence is about to break.

CHAPTER 3

THE NIGHT SHIFT: WHEN GOD SHOWS UP IN THE DARK

The God Who Avoids Palaces and Finds Pastures

The Surprise of Divine Priority

If humanity were writing the script of the
  Messiah's arrival—
We would expect the
  grand announcement to go to:

A king in a palace.
A priest in the temple.
A scholar in a library.
A general in a fortress.

Someone with influence.
Someone with reputation.
Someone with power.

But God almost never introduces Himself
Where the world expects Him.

He doesn't follow protocol.
He doesn't bow to prestige.
He doesn't court the important.
He doesn't audition for relevance.

When the God of the universe decides to
    reveal His greatest miracle,
He bypasses government, religion, and
    royalty—
And chooses …

Shepherds.

Who Shepherds Really Were

Shepherds were not charming nativity
    characters—
Wearing Hollywood-coordinated robes.

They were:

The lowest economic class;
Considered ceremonially unclean;
Viewed as thieves by society;
Rejected as witnesses in legal courts;
Assigned to the lowest, loneliest job;
Living outside the city walls;
Sleeping outdoors, exposed to danger.

The rabbis wrote in the Talmud:

"There is no more despised occupation
    in the world—
Than that of a shepherd."

Yet THESE are the men Heaven chose.

Not the priests with their polished rituals.
Not the philosophers with their polished
    thoughts.
Not the kings with their polished crowns.

God chooses people society ignores.

Because Heaven isn't impressed
With what impresses the world.

The Hillside of the Forgotten

A moon hanging over a rugged landscape.
A few tired shepherds huddled near a small
fire.
Sheep scattered across shadowy hills.
Cold wind blowing over worn cloaks.
Faces weathered, eyes heavy, hands
calloused—
The world sleeps behind them.
The city lights flicker in the distance.
Their names unknown.
Their work unnoticed.
Their value uncelebrated.

Yet—
This is the exact ground
Where Heaven is about to touch Earth.

The Night Shift

The shepherds were working the night
shift.

Not because they wanted to—
but because someone had to.

And isn't that a picture of life?

Night shift seasons are:

When you're awake while the world sleeps.
When you carry responsibilities no one
	sees.
When you fight battles no one knows
	about.
When you feel forgotten, unseen,
	undervalued.
When everyone else rests while you
	struggle to stay awake.

There are night shifts of the soul, too:

Nights of anxiety.
Nights of grief.
Nights of confusion.
Nights of spiritual drought.
Nights of hidden struggle.
Nights of waiting.
Nights of heartbreak.
Nights when God feels silent.

And yet—

God always shows up in the night.

Abraham heard God at night.
Jacob wrestled with God at night.
Samuel heard God call his name at night.
Daniel received visions at night.
Jesus was born at night.

Heaven tends to move—
When Earth least expects it.

The Silent Dialogue of the Shepherds

Let's imagine this night more vividly.

One shepherd pokes at the fire.
Another counts sheep in the shadows.
Another rubs his arms to stay warm.

They talk quietly:

"Think God still remembers us?"
"I haven't felt Him in years …"
"My father used to tell me stories of
    miracles…"

The voices continue:

"I wonder if Messiah will ever come."
"Maybe the prophets were wrong."
"Maybe Heaven forgot us."

It is the sound of many hearts today—
Tired, doubtful, wondering if God sees their
    night.

They didn't know, couldn't
    possibly guess—
That their quiet complaints
    were about to be interrupted—
By the loudest sound Heaven had made
    in centuries.

When Ordinary Men Meet Extraordinary Glory

The Bible says simply:

"And suddenly …"

Heaven rarely schedules miracles.
Heaven interrupts.

The shepherds are half asleep when the
    atmosphere changes.

The wind stops.
The air thickens.

A brightness appears—
    but not like fire …
    not like moonlight …
    not like lightning.

Something otherworldly.
Something alive.
Something holy.

Suddenly the sky—
The same sky they had stared
    at every night—
Rips open like a veil being torn asunder
    from the bottom to the top.

Light bursts forth.

Not a glow.
Not a shimmer.
Not a sparkle.

A GLORY.

A glory that has not touched
    Earth like this—

Since the day Solomon dedicated
    the Temple.

A glory so overwhelming that
    grown men collapse in terror.

A glory that turns night into day
    and day into worship.

The Explosion of Glory

A black sky transformed into blinding
    brilliance.
An angel, radiant and terrifying,
    descending like a comet of living light.
The shepherds shielding their eyes, falling
    to their knees, trembling.

Shadows fleeing.
Sheep frozen in awe.
Light saturating the air—

Not *illuminating* the world—

Saturating it.

The Angel Declares a Word
That Redefines History

And then the angel speaks the first Divine
    Message Earth has heard in 400 years:

"Fear not."

Of all the things Heaven could begin with—

Judgment?
Correction?
Prophecy?
Warning?
Instruction?

No.

Heaven's first words after centuries of
    silence were:

"Don't be afraid."

Because Heaven knows what
    Earth feels.
It knows fear keeps people from
    hearing God.
Fear keeps people from
    approaching Him.

Fear keeps people from
    believing Him.

After fear is broken,
    revelation can flow.

And here it comes—

"I bring you good news ..."

Not bad news.
Not heavy news.
Not condemning news.

"... of great joy ..."

Not ordinary joy.
Not seasonal joy.
Not thin joy.

But GREAT joy.
Mega joy.
Overflowing joy.

"... which shall be for all people."

Not just the rich.
Not just the righteous.

Not just the religious.
Not just the respected.

For ALL people.

Bethlehem's miracle was never meant to
stay in Bethlehem.

It was meant to shake the world.

Heaven Doubles Down

Before the shepherds can catch their
breath,
Heaven overwhelms them again:

"Suddenly there was with the angel
A multitude of the heavenly host."

Not a choir.

An ARMY.
A HOST.
A celestial BATTALION.

Thousands upon thousands—
possibly millions—
Filling every inch of sky.

This is the moment Heaven has been
  waiting for since Eden's tragic fall.

The angels who watched humanity break
  now watch humanity's salvation begin.

And they shout—
Not whisper, not sing politely—

SHOUT:

"Glory to God in the highest,
And on earth peace,
Goodwill toward men!"

The silence that lasted four centuries
  is now replaced—

By a ROAR—

That will echo for eternity.

CHAPTER 4

WHEN THE SKY CAUGHT FIRE

The Night Heaven Refused to Whisper

A Night Like Any Other … Until It Wasn't

The shepherds thought it was a typical night.

Cold.
Quiet.
Uneventful.
Predictable.

Their only goals:

Keep the sheep alive.
Stay awake.

Stay warm.
Survive the night.

But history doesn't announce itself.
Destiny never knocks politely.
Breakthrough rarely schedules
    appointments.

Heaven moves *"suddenly."*

And *suddenly*
The *ordinary*
Became *extraordinary*.

The *natural*
Became *supernatural*.

The *night*
Became *neon with glory*.

The First Flash of Glory

The shepherds blink.

Once.
Twice.

And then—

A flash.

Not a flash like lightning—
Which cracks and then disappears.

This light STAYS.

It does not flicker.
It does not fade.
It EXPANDS.

And the Bible says:

"The glory of the Lord shone round about
them." (Luke 2:9)

Not before them.
Not above them.
Not beside them.

AROUND them.

Meaning—

They were completely surrounded—
encircled; immersed in glory.

Like a ring of Heaven's fire hugging the
earth.

Like God Himself stepped into the night
And turned the hills into a sanctuary.

Encircled by Glory

A dark hillside illuminated
By a perfect sphere of heavenly light.

The shepherds engulfed in radiance.

No shadows remain.
Every blade of grass shimmering.
Their faces reflecting astonishment and
　　fear.

The sheep glowing in the spill of Divine
　　Presence.

Heaven forming a literal circle—
　　a crown—around ordinary men.

The Angel of the Lord Stood
Before Them

Unlike the angels in greeting cards—

This angel is not soft,
Not subtle,
Not delicate.

He is terrifying in his Holiness.

His presence feels like a storm wrapped in
sunlight.
Like a thousand suns compressed into a
single beam.
Like fire wearing a face.

Every molecule in the air responds to him.

The winds bow.
The earth stills.
The shepherds collapse under the weight
of his glory.

Because before an angel speaks—
An angel *is* a message.

And Heaven's first message is always …

Glory before *words*.

The Shepherds' Reaction

Their hearts pound.
Their hands shake.
Their knees buckle.

One shepherd clutches his chest.
Another shields his face.
One falls fully to the ground.
Another stammers:

"We're going to die."
"This is the end."
"God has come to judge us."
"We are undone …"

Because when holiness appears to
    humanity,
Our first instinct is fear—
Not because God is harsh,
But because God is overwhelming.

But Heaven's messenger is ready.
The first Divine Word after 400 years is:

"Fear not."

Fear has to be silenced—
   before joy can be heard.

Fear has to be addressed—
   before revelation can be received.

Fear has to bow—
   before the Gospel can rise.

I Bring You Good News

The angel's voice is not a whisper—
It is a vibration in the air.
A resonance that touches bone and soul.

His next words reshape the world:

"I bring you good news of great joy ..."

Not seasonal joy.
Not sentimental joy.
Not circumstantial joy.

But megawatt, earth-shattering, destiny-
   altering joy.

Joy not rooted in what you feel—
   but in what God has done.

Joy not based on emotion—
    but on incarnation.

Joy not founded in stability—
    but in salvation.

This is the kind of joy
That can survive a storm,
Outlast a valley,
And break the chains of the mind.

Which Shall Be for All People

The angel does not say:

"To the rich only."
"To the educated only."
"To the religious only."
"To the powerful only."

He says:

"ALL people."

Shepherds included.
Sinners included.
Outcasts included.

Gentiles included.
You included.

Bethlehem is the birthplace
of universal invitation.

The manger is the doorway
for global grace.

The Second Invasion — The Sky Rips Open Again

Now the text shifts from miracle
to MULTITUDE.

Luke writes:

"Suddenly there was with the angel

A multitude of the heavenly host ..."

The Greek word for "host" (στρατιά) literally means:

AN ARMY.

Heaven doesn't send a small ensemble.
It sends a battalion.

Not a choir of sweet-voiced cherubs—
But a military rank of glory-warriors.

This is not a lullaby.
This is a war cry.

The sky fills—
Not with stars,
But with soldiers.

Legions of angels—
Stretching beyond the horizon,
Layer upon layer of burning glory.

The shepherds do not see a few angels—
They see a HEAVENLY ARMY
Surrounding the heavens
As far as the eye can see.

The Sky Catching Fire

An ocean of angels layered across the sky
   like living flames.
Wings of lightning, eyes of fire, armor
   shimmering with holiness.

The entire sky transformed into a
supernatural battlefield—

FILLED WITH WORSHIP.

The shepherds trembling beneath the
burning canopy of Heaven.

Every star swallowed by glory.

Every darkness fleeing.

THE NIGHT SKY AFLAME WITH GOD.

The First Heavenly Worship Service in Centuries

Then the angels ROAR.

This is not singing as we think of singing.
This is worship in its purest, rawest, most
unfiltered form.

A frequency that shakes atoms.
A resonance that moves mountains.
A sound that pierces the veil between
realms.

They declare:

"Glory to God in the highest!"

Heaven gives God glory
At the highest possible decibel—
Frequency.
Intensity.
Magnitude.

It is glory uncontainable.
Glory unrestrained.
Glory unleashed.

Then—

"… and on earth peace …"

Peace not as the world gives.
Not a peace of calm circumstances.
Not political peace.
Not emotional quiet.

But shalom—
Wholeness.
Restoration.
Healing.
Reconciliation.

Peace on earth
Because Heaven just touched earth.

Peace on earth
Because God came near.

Peace on earth
Because a Savior has been born.

"… goodwill toward men."

Goodwill equals *divine delight*.
God is not angry—
He is pleased to rescue humanity.

This moment is the revelation
Of God's heart toward mankind.

He does not come to condemn—
But to redeem.

Not to crush—
But to carry.

Not to distance—
But to draw near.

The Heavens Thunder, and the Earth Trembles

The shepherds are undone.

One screams.
One weeps.
One kneels.

One covers his ears—
    overwhelmed.
Another reaches toward the sky—
    trembling.

Their hearts feel like they are being
    rewritten.
Their souls feel like they are being reborn.

Because once you see Heaven worship—
you can never go back to ordinary life.

CHAPTER 5

HEAVEN SPOKE. EARTH SLEPT.

*The Tragedy of a World Too
Distracted to Hear God*

The Most Haunting Contrast in Scripture

Luke 2, the Nativity—
One of the loudest nights in the
   Bible.

Heaven is singing.
Angels are shouting.
The sky is burning.
The glory is blazing.
Revelation is exploding.
Prophecy is unfolding.

Divinity is descending.
Eternity is speaking.

And yet—Earth is sleeping.

Bethlehem snored under the brightest sky
    it had ever seen.
Jerusalem slumbered under the most
    important announcement in history.
Kings dreamed while angels declared war
    songs of peace.
Priests rested while the Messiah they
    prayed for lay three miles away.
The innkeeper slept while God slept in his
    stable.

Heaven spoke—
Earth slept.

The Sleeping City

Bethlehem under the glow of supernatural
    light.
Blue twilight, rooftops glowing, windows
    dark.

Shadows still.
Streets empty.

The sky ablaze with millions of angels
Unseen by the city below.

Heaven thunderous—
Earth unconscious.

The People Who Missed God

The innkeeper didn't reject Jesus—
He simply didn't *recognize* Him.

The inn was full.
The schedule was full.
The night was full.
His life was full.

Fullness made him blind.

God was at his doorstep.
He was too busy to notice.

Herod wasn't asleep—
He was too awake, too paranoid,

Too self-protective to perceive God's
move.

Fear made him blind.

The Priests knew the Scriptures.
They knew the prophecies.
They knew the birthplace.
They even told Herod where the Messiah
would be born.

Knowledge made them blind.

They researched the Messiah
But did not seek the Messiah.

Jerusalem was the holy city.
The city of the temple.
The city of worship.

But religion made them blind.

They went through the motions
While missing the miracle
Unfolding beside them.

The Generational Message
We Must Hear

This is the tragedy of the Bethlehem night:

The ones who were SURE they'd notice God … didn't.

The ones who didn't think God noticed THEM … saw everything.

The shepherds saw Him.
The forgotten heard Him.
The humble encountered Him.
The overlooked received Revelation.

Heaven's pattern has not changed.

The Parallel of Our
Generation

We are living in a culture overwhelmed with noise:

Endless notifications.
Constant streams of information.
24/7 news cycles.

Social media overload.
Political shouting matches.
Pressure to produce.
Addiction to distraction.
Obsession with speed.
Entertainment gluttony.
Spiritual numbness disguised as busyness.

We are the most connected generation in
    history—
And the least attentive to Heaven.

We are the loudest generation—
And the least able to discern God's voice.

We are the most informed—
And the least transformed.

We scroll more than we seek.
We post more than we pray.
We speak more than we listen.
We worry more than we worship.
We react more than we reflect.

And Heaven is speaking—
    right now—
But we are drowning in our own volume.

The Modern Noise

A person sitting in darkness illuminated by
    a glowing phone—

Around them swirl:

Notifications.
Texts.
Emails.
Icons.
Social feeds.
Advertisements.
Breaking news.
Opinions.

Yet behind them stands a radiant figure—

Christ—
    speaking softly.

The person cannot hear Him.
The noise is too loud.

The Problem Is Not God's Volume — It's Our Attention

We often pray:

"Lord, speak to me!"

But Heaven responds:

"My child, I have been speaking.
You're just too busy to hear Me."

We desire signs, wonders, angelic
    encounters—

But we ignore Scripture.
We ignore conviction.
We ignore the nudge of the Spirit.
We ignore the whisper during worship.
We ignore the tug in our chest that won't
    go away.

We want God to shout—
But He wants us to listen.

He is not silent—
We are distracted.

He is not distant—
We are inattentive.

He is not hiding—
We are scrolling.

Heaven spoke—
Earth slept.

And Heaven is speaking—
But Earth is spiritually
    asleep.

The Call to Wake Up

Paul writes:

"Awake, O sleeper ..."

He is not rebuking sinners—
He is awakening the church.

We cannot afford to sleep.
It's the greatest move of God in our
    lifetime.

We cannot snore through revival.
We cannot nap through visitation.

We cannot dream while Heaven downloads
    destiny.

This is the hour to:

Wake up your worship.
Wake up your discernment.
Wake up your hunger.
Wake up your prayer life.
Wake up your spirit.
Wake up your sensitivity to God.
Wake up your awareness of Heaven.

Because Heaven is speaking—

And those who are awake
    will hear Him.

CHAPTER 6

IF HEAVEN BROKE ITS SILENCE TODAY

Would We Even Notice?

The Question That Shakes the Soul

If Heaven broke its silence tonight—
Right now—
In your home,
In your car,
In your heart,

Would you notice?

The shepherds noticed.
But Bethlehem didn't.

Not because the shepherds were smarter.
Not because they were holier.
Not because they were spiritually elite.

It's because the shepherds were *listening*
while Bethlehem was *sleeping*.

The shepherds were *awake* in the night
while the city felt *secure* in the dark.

They weren't distracted.
They weren't entertained.
They weren't scrolling.
They weren't racing.

They were simply present.

So, Heaven found them.

What Would God Have to Do to Get Your Attention?

A sign?
A dream?
A miracle?
A tragedy?
A whisper?

A shout?
A burning bush?
A lightning bolt?
A sky filled with angels?

Here's the truth:

God speaks far more often than we think—

We just aren't listening as deeply as He is
    speaking.

The Many Ways Heaven Speaks

God is breaking silence in your life
    right now—

Through:

Scripture.

Not just ink on paper
But Heaven-breathed truth.
Verses you "stumble upon" are not
    accidents—
They are divine appointments.

Conviction.

When your spirit tightens,
When your conscience stirs,
That's not guilt—
That's God guarding you.

Worship.

The song you cry through.
The moment you feel peace descend.
The lyric that hits too close.
God speaks in the atmosphere of
adoration.

Prayer Impressions.

That nudge.
That whisper.
That idea that didn't come from you.
That weight that sits on your heart.
That prompting that won't let go.

Peace That Makes No Sense

The kind that shows up in storms.
The kind that silences anxiety.
Peace is not passive—

It's Heaven's language of
    guidance.

Holy Discontent

When you can't shake
    the feeling—
That God wants more from you …
That's not frustration—
That's God calling.

Desire for Holiness

When suddenly sin tastes bitter …
When righteousness pulls on you …
This is Heaven—
Reshaping your appetites.

People God Sends

Mentors.
Strangers.
Sermons.
Friends who speak truth.
Encounters that seem random—
But are supernatural
    interventions.

Closed Doors

God speaks through NO just as loudly
As He speaks through YES.

Pain, Trials, and Valleys

God never wastes pain.
He shouts in storms
What we ignore in the sunshine.

The Whisper in the Thunder

A storm scene—
Lightning, waves, roaring winds.
And in the very center,
A faint, glowing whisper
Hovering near the heart of a kneeling
    figure.

Though everything is loud—
The whisper is stronger.

It is the still, small voice
That Elijah heard on Horeb—
The same voice
Still speaking today.

The Tragedy of Modern Spiritual Deafness

We ask God to speak …
But we live at a volume
One that makes it nearly impossible
To hear Him.

We want guidance
Without stillness.

We want revelation
Without meditation.

We want clarity
Without consecration.

We want miracles
Without margins.

We want Divine direction
In a life that has no room for Divine
    interruption.

And Heaven cannot compete
With the volume we choose.

God refuses to shout over idols.
He refuses to compete with distractions.

He doesn't yell—
Because He whispers.

And whispers require intimacy.

The Gentle Language of God

Heaven's voice is not fragile—
Just intimate.

He speaks in ways that require you to:

Lean in.
Slow down.
Become quiet.
Pay attention.
Surrender distraction.
Elevate hunger.

He whispers because He wants you close,
Not because He is weak.

He wants relationship,
Not performance.

He wants conversation,
Not consultation.

He wants communion,
Not convenience.

The Inner Battle for Stillness

The greatest spiritual warfare of our
    generation
Is not against demons—
It's against distraction.

The enemy doesn't need to destroy you
If he can distract you.

He doesn't need to tempt you
If he can deafen you.

He doesn't need to persecute you
If he can preoccupy you.

Satan is a strategist.

He knows:

A distracted Christian
    is a disarmed Christian.

A busy Christian
    is a spiritually brittle Christian.

A constantly stimulated Christian
   is a shallow Christian.

A hurried Christian
   cannot hear Heaven.

The Competing Voices

Two figures stand in the mind:

One is Christ—
   lit by holy fire, speaking a soft word.

The other—
   a whirlwind of:

Screens.
Voices.
Alerts.
Clocks.
Deadlines.
Noise.

Christ speaks once.
The noise speaks constantly.

The battle is not who is louder—
But who is listened to.

How To Know When God Is Speaking to You

You will know Heaven is breaking silence
when:

Your spirit feels pulled toward prayer,
You feel a holy dissatisfaction with sin.
You feel peace guiding you into difficult
obedience.
A Scripture "comes alive" inside you.
You feel drawn toward worship.
You sense conviction and correction.
You feel God inviting you into deeper
surrender.
A sermon feels like it was written for you.
A thought comes that carries weight and
holiness.
Your heart becomes tender in God's
presence.

These are not emotions.

They are encounters.

Revelation. A Divine Invitation.

This is Heaven breaking silence inside you.

The Tender Truth: You Are Being Called

If you feel God tugging …
If you feel stirred …
If something in you awakens when you
     read this …
If your heart feels warm or heavy …
If your spirit feels illuminated …
If tears rise for no reason …
If conviction is stirring …
If hunger is awakening …

You are not losing your mind.
You are being called.

Heaven is breaking silence—
Not in the sky,
But in *you*.

CHAPTER 7

THE REVOLUTION OF REDEMPTION

*How the Cry of a Baby Became the
Roar That Shattered Hell*

The Baby Grew

The cry that pierced Bethlehem
Did not remain a whisper.

The tiny hands that reached for Mary
Would one day reach for a cross.

The soft breath that fogged the cold night
  air—
Would one day command storms and
  demons and death itself.

And the eyes that blinked open in a
    manger—
Would one day look upon Jerusalem and
    weep.

Jesus did not stay in Bethlehem.

He grew …

He learned.
He worked.
He walked.
He taught.
He healed.
He delivered.

He carried Heaven inside human skin.

And everywhere He went—
He broke silence.

He broke the silence over:

Lepers no one touched.
Women no one honored.
Sinners no one forgave.
Children no one valued.
Outcasts no one saw.

He spoke the words—
Human hearts had forgotten
  how to hear.

Words like:

"Follow Me."
"Be healed."
"Your sins are forgiven."
"Fear not."
"It is I."
"Come unto Me."
"I am the Light of the world."
"I am the Good Shepherd."
"I am the Resurrection and the Life."

Every word Jesus spoke
Was Heaven breaking silence again.

But the silence wasn't finished.

The Night the Sky Went Dark

The same Jesus who arrived under a bright
  sky—
Would one day hang under a dark one.

The Light of the world
Stood between two thieves
As the world mocked Him.

Heaven had once exploded with glory at
    His birth—
Now Heaven is watching quietly as Earth
    crucifies its Messiah.

The angels who once filled the sky with
    praise—
Now clench their fists in holy anguish.

Michael stands with sword drawn,
Waiting for the Father's command—
But the Father gives none.

Because this silence is different.
This silence is part of the plan.

This silence is not Heaven ignoring—
    but Heaven redeeming.

The Lamb is taking humanity's place.

The Innocent becomes the guilty.
The Perfect becomes sin.
The Sinless One becomes every broken

thing—
That will ever shatter the human heart.

And then—
The One who first broke Heaven's silence
    with His infant cry—
Breaks silence again with a sound
    that shakes both Heaven and hell.

It Is Finished!

Tetelestai.

It was the cry that rewrote eternity.

When He cried those words—

The veil tore.
The earth shook.
Tombs opened.
Hell panicked.
Demons screamed.
Angels bowed.
Prophecy aligned.
Redemption ignited.

The silence between God and humanity
Was forever shattered.

This shout is the final note
    in Heaven's strategy
That began in the throne room
    and descended into Bethlehem.

"It is finished."

The roar ends
    the tyranny of silence.

The Shout That Split the Ages

The cross silhouetted against a blackened
    sky.
Lightning framing Christ's body.
The veil in the temple ripping from bottom
    to top.
Angels watching in both agony and awe.
The earth cracking.
Light bursting from the torn veil.
A shockwave rippling from Calvary across
    time.

The World Tried to Silence Him

They took His body.
They wrapped it.
They buried it.
They sealed it.
They stationed guards around it.

Earth tried to end Heaven's message
    by burying the Messenger.

Hell whispered:

"Finally.
The voice is quiet.
The Word is dead.
The silence has returned."

But Hell forgot something:

Silence is where God prepares His
    greatest miracles.

The womb was silent before Bethlehem.
The tomb was silent before resurrection.

God does His best work
In places that feel quiet.

The Second Great Breaking of Silence

Then—on the third day—
Heaven inhaled again.

And with one angelic assignment,
God shattered silence eternally.

A quake.
A flash.
A stone rolling like paper.
Soldiers collapsing like dead men.
A tomb opening like a mouth ready to
    proclaim truth.

And an angel proclaiming words
That Hell never wanted to hear.

He Is Not Here — He Is Risen!

The silence of death
    was broken.

The silence of fear
    was broken.

The silence of hopelessness
    was broken.

The silence of sin
    was broken.

The silence of humanity's separation from
    God was shattered forever.

When the Tomb Could Not Hold a Voice

The stone mid-roll,
Pushed by blinding angelic light.

The grave bursting with radiance.
Soldiers falling backward in terror.

Angels surrounding the entrance
    in triumph.
The dawn breaking over an empty tomb—

The Light of the World returning
    to the world.

The Revolution of Redemption

Heaven broke silence at His birth.
Heaven broke silence at His cross.
Heaven broke silence at His resurrection.

And now—

Heaven breaks silence
Every time a sinner repents,
Every time a heart surrenders,
Every time a soul is healed,
Every time a prayer is answered,
Every time worship fills the air,
Every time the Gospel is preached,
Every time Jesus speaks through His Spirit.

What Jesus started in Bethlehem,
He completed at Calvary
And empowered at the empty tomb.

You serve a God
Who refuses to stay silent.

You serve a Christ
Who speaks resurrection into dead places.

You serve a Savior
Who shouts louder than the grave.

Chapter 8

HEAVEN IS STILL SPEAKING

God Broke the Silence in Bethlehem.
He Broke It Again at the Tomb.
And He Is Breaking It Again in You.

The God Who Refuses to Remain Quiet

Heaven did not break silence once.
Not twice.
But continually.

Bethlehem was the first crack.
Calvary was the fracture.
The Resurrection was the shattering.

And since then—
Heaven has been speaking

Into every generation,
Every culture,
Every heart that dares to listen.

God is not a distant deity.
God is not an absentee Father.
God is not an ancient echo growing weaker
with time.

He is the ever-present, ever-speaking,
ever-moving, ever-reaching God.

He is Emmanuel.

God WITH us.

Not God *was* with us.
Not God *used to be* with us.
Not God *might be* with us.

God *IS* with us.

Here.
Now.
In this moment.
In your struggle.
In your silence.

The Big Question: What Silence Do You Need Him to Break?

Silence can take many forms:

The silence of unanswered prayers.
The silence of depression.
The silence of anxiety.
The silence of heartbreak.
The silence of betrayal.
The silence of loneliness.
The silence of waiting.
The silence of disappointment.
The silence of shame.
The silence of grief.
The silence of spiritual numbness.
The silence of feeling forgotten by God.

Everyone carries a silence.

Some silences are loud.
Some silences are painful.
Some silences are suffocating.

But Heaven specializes in breaking silence.

The same God who broke it for Israel,
Who broke it for the shepherds,

Who broke it for Mary,
Who broke it for Joseph,
Who broke it for the world—

Wants to break it for you.

The Hand That Breaks the Silence

A person kneeling in a dark room,
Their head bowed,
Their hands clasped.

From Heaven:

A beam of radiant light
    touches their chest—
Shattering the darkness around them
    like glass breaking in slow motion.

The light forms the shape of a voice
    going forth—
Heaven speaking into
    human silence.

Heaven Is Breaking Silence in You When …

You feel conviction rising.
Tears come unexpectedly.
Your heart feels stirred.
Your mind begins to open.
A Scripture comes alive.
Worship hits deeper.
Peace settles where panic lived.
Hunger for God awakens.
You sense "There's more."
You feel God calling your name.

These are NOT coincidences.

These are NOT emotions.

These are NOT psychological phenomena.

These are not the result of music, lighting,
    or atmosphere.

These are the fingerprints of God
    pressing on your soul.

This is Heaven whispering,
    "I'm still speaking to you."

When God Breaks Silence, Miracles Break Loose

When Heaven speaks—
Darkness trembles.

When God whispers—
Storms bow.

When God calls—
Chains fall.

When God declares—
Dead things wake up.

When God breathes—
Dry bones rise.

When God commands—
Demons flee.

When God sings—
The universe harmonizes.

When God breaks silence—
Your life will NEVER stay the same.

The Declaration You Must Make

Lift your hands—
Lift your heart—
Lift your expectation—
And declare with authority:

"Lord, break the silence *in me*."

Break the silence of confusion.
Break the silence of fear.
Break the silence of doubt.
Break the silence of spiritual apathy.
Break the silence of unanswered
    questions.
Break the silence of old wounds.
Break the silence of shame.
Break the silence of generational pain.
Break the silence of disappointment.

"Lord, break the silence *for me*."

Break the silence around my family.
Break the silence around my calling.
Break the silence around my purpose.
Break the silence around my future.

Break the silence around my prayers.
Break the silence around my breakthrough.

"Lord, break the silence *through me*."

Let me be Your vessel.
Let me carry Your voice.
Let me declare Your word.
Let me speak into darkness.
Let me announce hope to the hopeless.
Let me bring peace into chaos.
Let me shine light into someone's night.

When Heaven breaks silence in you—
Heaven begins breaking silence
    THROUGH you.

What Happens When You Respond to His Voice

When Heaven speaks and you respond:

Your identity shifts.
Your purpose awakens.
Your calling becomes clear.
Your heart becomes tender.

Your spirit becomes alive.
Your vision expands.
Your fear loses power.
Your faith gains momentum.
Your worship deepens.
Your mind becomes renewed.
Your destiny unfolds.

And suddenly—
The silence that once suffocated you
Becomes the soil where miracles grow.

This Is Not Just a Story — It Is an Invitation

The night Heaven broke its silence
Was not a one-time event.

It was the beginning
Of an eternal conversation.

Between God and man.
Between Heaven and Earth.
Between Creator and creation.
Between Father and child.

Heaven is still speaking.

To nations.
To churches.
To families.
To generations.
To YOU.

This book is not the end—
It is the beginning of God speaking afresh
    into your soul.

And you will walk out of this moment
Not silent,
Not broken,
Not forgotten—

But awakened.

Awakened to your calling.
Awakened to His voice.
Awakened to His presence.
Awakened to His purpose.

SERMON OUTLINES

WHEN HEAVEN BREAKS THE SILENCE

Text: Luke 2:8–14

1. God's Silence Is Not God's Absence

   - 400 years of quiet

   - Silence as preparation

   - Heaven's timing

2. God Speaks to the Humble First

   - Shepherds as Heaven's audience

   - God bypasses pride

   - God meets us in night seasons

3. When God Speaks, Fear Must Bow

   - "Fear not!"

- Fear blocks hearing
- Fear melts in God's presence

4. The Gospel Is Mega-Joy for ALL People

- Good news for the broken
- Joy that survives storms
- Salvation's inclusivity

5. Heaven Still Speaks Today

- Through Scripture
- Through conviction
- Through worship
- Through peace
- Through the Spirit's whisper

Call to Response:

"Lord, break the silence in me."

THE NIGHT THE SKY CAUGHT FIRE!

Text: Luke 2:8–14

1. When Heaven Shows Up, the Ordinary EXPLODES With Glory

- Shepherds → revival candidates
- Glory surrounding them
- God turning night into day

2. Hell Cannot Stop a Word From Heaven

- 400 years of silence broken
- Darkness interrupted
- Glory invading the enemy's territory

3. GOOD TIDINGS! GREAT JOY! FOR ALL PEOPLE!

- Joy breaks chains
- Joy breaks curses
- Joy breaks oppression

4. When Heaven Speaks, Angels ROAR!

- The host filling the sky

- Heaven declaring war against darkness

- Peace released over Earth

5. If Heaven Spoke Then—Heaven Is Speaking NOW!

- Breakthrough in your night

- Miracles in your darkness

- God is about to invade your situation

Altar Call:

This is your "suddenly" moment.
Heaven is breaking silence *right now.*

EXEGESIS OF REVELATION IN LUKE 2:8–14

1. The Socio-Historical Context of Shepherds

- Marginalized class
- Theological symbolism of David
- Shepherds as Israel-in-miniature

2. Angelology and Luke's Narrative Framework

- Angelic visitation patterns
- "Angel of the Lord" identity
- Fear and divine encounter motifs

3. Greek Analysis of Key Phrases

- "Megas chara" (great joy)
- "Pasin" (all people)
- "Stratia" (army)
- "Eirene" (peace, shalom fullness)

4. Theological Themes in the Announcement

- Incarnation

- Universality of salvation

- Heaven-Earth interaction

- Revelation after silence

5. Literary Structure and Prophetic Fulfillment

- Intertextual links to Isaiah 9

- Messianic expectation

- Covenantal continuity

WHERE HAS HEAVEN FELT SILENT IN YOUR LIFE?

"My God, my God, why have you abandoned me?" — Psalm 22:1

There are seasons when God's quietness feels like abandonment—but in Scripture, silence is preparation.

Reflection Questions:

- What area of your life feels the most uncertain right now?

- Where do you feel you have prayed without answers?

- What emotions—fear, frustration, confusion—rise up around this silence?

- Is there a past season where God was silent—but later you realized He was working?

Journaling Prompts:

- Describe a moment where Heaven felt distant.

- Write what you *wish* God would say to you in this silence.

- Now write what you *know* to be true about Him despite it.

Scripture Voice:

"Be still and know that I am God." — Psalm 46:10

Prayer:

Lord, teach me to trust You in silence.
Let Your quiet become my confidence,
not my fear.

Prophetic Whisper:

"I am not absent.
I am aligning things you cannot see."

WHAT NIGHT SEASON HAS GOD TRUSTED YOU TO WALK THROUGH?

"Weeping may last through the night, but joy comes with the morning." — *Psalm 30:5*

Night seasons are not punishments— they are classrooms.

Reflection Questions:

- What has been your darkest "night season"?

- What did you learn about yourself in that place?

- How did God sustain you even when you didn't feel Him?

- What strengths were forged in your night?

Journaling Prompts:

- Describe a night season from your past with complete honesty.

- What parts of that season still affect you today?

- What would you tell someone else walking that same path?

Scripture Voice:

"The people who walk in darkness will see a great light." — Isaiah 9:2

Prayer:

Lord, You are the God who shows up in the night. Turn every dark place into a place of revelation.

Prophetic Whisper:

"Your night is not the end—it is the birthplace of My glory."

HOW IS GOD SPEAKING TO YOU LATELY — EVEN IN SUBTLE WAYS?

"My sheep listen to my voice; I know them, and they follow me." — John 10:27

God rarely shouts.
He usually whispers.

Reflection Questions:

- When was the last time you felt a "nudge" or inner prompting?

- Has Scripture felt unusually alive recently?

- Has conviction sharpened?

- Have you felt peace in places that once carried fear?

Journaling Prompts:

- List all the possible ways God may have spoken to you this month.

- Write down any Scripture that keeps returning to your heart.

- Describe a moment when you felt God's presence without words.

Scripture Voice:

"Speak, your servant is listening." — 1 Samuel 3:10

Prayer:

Lord, tune my ears to Your frequency. Help me notice what You're whispering.

Prophetic Whisper:

"I have been speaking—you are learning to hear Me again."

IN WHAT "SHEPHERD PLACE" DO YOU FEEL OVERLOOKED?

"People judge by outward appearance, but the Lord looks at the heart." — 1 Samuel 16:7

The shepherd field is not punishment— it is preparation.

Reflection Questions:

- Where do you feel undervalued?

- Who has overlooked you or misunderstood your calling?

- How might God be using this "field season" to shape you?

Journaling Prompts:

- Write about the place or season where you've felt most unseen.

- Describe how God might be forming humility or character in that space.

- Identify what responsibilities in this season are actually sacred assignments.

Scripture Voice:

"Humble yourselves under the mighty power of God, and at the right time he will lift you up in honor." — 1 Peter 5:6

Prayer:

Lord, thank You for the fields. Thank You for choosing me even when others do not.

Prophetic Whisper:

"I see you. Your field is the doorway to your calling."

WHAT SILENCE ARE YOU ASKING GOD TO BREAK?

"Ask me and I will tell you remarkable secrets ..." — *Jeremiah 33:3*

This is your breakthrough question.

Reflection Questions:

- What is the #1 silence that weighs heaviest on your heart?

- How long have you carried it?

- What will it look like when Heaven breaks this silence?

- How will your faith respond?

Journaling Prompts:

- Write the silence you want God to break in one bold sentence.

- Describe the miracle you long to see.

- Write a prayer as if the miracle has already happened.

Scripture Voice:

"For the word of God will never fail." — Luke 1:37

Prayer:

Break the silence, Lord—
in me, for me, through me.
I am ready for Your voice to shake my world.

Prophetic Whisper:

"The silence you fear is the silence I am filling."

WHAT HAS GOD BEEN BIRTHING IN YOU DURING THE SILENCE?

"For I am about to do something new. See, I have already begun! Do you not see it?"
— *Isaiah 43:19*

God uses silence to conceive things in us that noise would abort.

Reflection Questions:

- What dream, idea, or calling has quietly grown inside you?

- What spiritual hunger has awakened?

- What character traits have deepened?

Journaling Prompts:

- Describe something new being birthed in you.

- What scares you about it?

- What excites you about it?

Scripture Voice:

"And I am certain that God, who began the good work within you, will continue his work until it is finally finished on the day when Christ Jesus returns." — Philippians 1:6

Prayer:

Lord, thank You for what You are forming in me.
Give me courage to carry it to birth.

Prophetic Whisper:

"The quiet work is the deepest work."

HOW WILL YOU RESPOND WHEN HEAVEN SPEAKS?

"Today when you hear his voice, don't harden your hearts." — *Hebrews 3:15*

God speaks—but we decide how to respond.

Reflection Questions:

- Will you act when God nudges?

- Will you obey even when you don't understand?

- Will you trust Him even when you cannot trace Him?

Journaling Prompts:

- Write the commitment you are ready to make.

- Write the step of obedience you've been afraid to take.

- Describe what a fully surrendered version of you looks like.

Scripture Voice:

"Here am I. Send me." — Isaiah 6:8

Prayer:

Lord, I will respond. Speak—and I will follow.

Prophetic Whisper:

"If you draw near, you will hear Me clearly."

THE FINAL REFLECTION
DECLARATION

Speak this aloud:

"Lord, break the silence IN me.
Break the silence FOR me.
Break the silence THROUGH me.
Let Heaven speak again … and let me
    never stop listening."

A Final Word

You can find Tim on the South Texas District website at www.stxag.org, on Facebook, or at his Houston office when he's not traveling his home state ministering in the churches across the South Texas District.

He'd be thrilled to connect with you and share stories of God's faithfulness.

Additional Books by

Tim R. Barker

If you liked this book, you may be interested in additional books Tim has written. Turn the page for a short description of each book. All are available on Amazon.

My *Jesus* Journey

This soul-building, introspective 4-book series reveals Tim's innermost heart on subjects that affect all of us, from Cooperation to Loyalty to The Truth of Salvation and more.

The books in this series include:

My Jesus Journey

My Jesus Journey: Crescendo

My Jesus Journey: Glissando

My Jesus Journey: Rhapsody

At *Your* Feet

In this book, you will read of God's favor and His redemption, for you are chosen and forgiven. In Jesus, you can find the rest you desire, for at His feet, His joy becomes whole.

Come to Jesus today. He holds His hand out to you.

From the Book of Hebrews
The Lord with Us

Do you have a relationship with Jesus? The rewards are great, but if we fail to heed the warnings in the Word, the consequences are also great.

Even if we call ourselves Christian, we must live according to God's will. The Lord is with us when we walk with Him. This is the message from the book of Hebrews.

Our Privilege of Joy

A Study of the Book of Philippians

Philippians is our blueprint from the Father, our plan for joy. It was written by the hand of Paul during his time in a Roman prison, but the voice is the Father's, entreating us to lift our hands in praise to Him, and to find joy even in the difficult parts of our lives.

NAMES OF GOD

Our name tells people who we are.

What about the name Christian? That's what the followers of Jesus call themselves. What information can people glean about us when we put a fish symbol on the bumper of our car, or we wear a cross around our neck? And, importantly, do our actions live up to their expectations?

This book is an in-depth teaching about the ten names of God.

THE VISION OF NEHEMIAH

GOD'S PLAN FOR RIGHTEOUS LIVING

The Book of Nehemiah reveals a vital truth that our instant society often overlooks. Determination can take us only so far in achieving the goals God has for today's Church.

Winning the lost for Christ takes preparation in both our time and our finances. We become the "right stuff" for achieving God's plan when we are willing to risk everything for Him.

GOD'S REVELATION AND YOUR FUTURE

The book of Revelation is first and foremost a revelation about Jesus, not just the future.

John reveals Christ as the King of Glory, the conqueror, the one in charge of history, the one who alone controls the future, controls the nations, controls all the universe! This is the Jesus who is coming!

The book of Revelation shows us the glorified Christ and the certainty of His ruling over all things. We are not stumbling toward an uncertain future, but we must be in fellowship with the King!

Truth, Love & Redemption

The Holy Spirit For Today

There is no greater empowerment for the Christian of today than to seek out the Holy Spirit. It was considered vital in the early days of Christendom. Now, many times it is pushed aside as "for then" and not "for now."

We are in greater need of the truth, love, and redemption that flows from an encounter with the Holy Spirit than ever before. The Scriptures tell us that our realization of our need for Christ flows from the Spirit. Even before we accept Christ, the Holy Spirit draws us to Him.

The Call of Ephesians

Building the Church of Today

Paul understood that legalism can become a hindrance to our Christian walk and that we must focus on Christ and Christ alone. When our faith hits the road, God is there with us. He challenges us to trust Him to walk at our side through every challenge we might face.

When we do, we become mighty warriors in God's army.

That's Paul's message in a nutshell, and it's vital we take it to heart.

The Twelve

Taking up the Mantle of Christ

Twelve men were chosen to fulfill Christ's legacy on the earth.

Eleven looked to Jesus for the answers to life's questions. One chose the world and the world failed him.

These men were as varied as the members of our modern church, at times at odds with one another, but forged by Jesus into a single unit that overcame everything the devil could throw at them. What lesson can we learn from them?

Our only option is to choose Christ.

END TIMES

Scripture provides us a timeline of events that signal that the end is coming soon.

1. The Church Age
2. The Rapture of the Church
3. The Tribulation
4. The Second Coming of Jesus Christ
5. The Millennium
6. The Great White Throne Judgment
7. New Heavens and New Earth

Follow along through each of these Biblical timeline events.

Anticipating the Return of Christ

Are we waiting or are we watching for His appearance in the skies? The difference is in being ready for His return and risking missing Him altogether.

This book covers six areas of preparation for the Return of Christ.

1. Waiting
2. Mindful
3. Joyful
4. Praying
5. Thanking
6. Faithful.

Are you anticipating Christ's return? I am.

I *Your* •nvitation • to *Christ*

Your Invitation to Christ guarantees six things. Once you accept Christ's invitation you can:

1. Rest. It's yours in the midst of whatever comes your way.

2. See. Your eyes are opened to the supernatural.

3. Follow. Christ is your only true leader.

4. Drink. The ambrosia of Jesus becomes yours.

5. Dine. You will find renewal in your fellowship with your Lord.

6. Inherit. The Kingdom will one day be yours. It's called Heaven.

Salvation comes through Christ. God desires our presence, and we draw closer to Him through our Lord and Savior, Jesus.

The Authentic Christian

Revealing Christ through the Fruit of the Spirit

How do we prove who we say we are?

What's the secret to how it's done?

Is it in appearance? Actions that portray honesty?

How do we live out our Christian example, prove that we are who we say we are? What's our authentication, our password, our photo ID?

That's what this book is about, how we can live a real and honest Christian life that reflects the truth of Jesus living through us.

When you finish this book, you will understand what it means to be an authentic Christian.

Unified Church

The world cries out for your leadership as a Christ-driven example of how to find security and safety in Him.

We must band together arm-in-arm, hand-in-hand, our thoughts, compassion, and commitment to each other linked for a common goal we all share: spreading the message of salvation to a world that desperately needs to see the example of Jesus lived out through committed believers.

This book will become a useful tool to focus your witness to those around you and strengthen your relationship to your family, your involvement in your local body of believers and your commitment to Christ.

Mighty Men of Courage

From the Bible

Joseph who was sold into slavery. Daniel faced the lion's den. Abraham saw few of the promises of God during his lifetime. Moses lived for four decades in disgrace, an apparent failure.

Elijah hid in the desert with the ravens for three years, and Paul was arrested for his faith and thrown in prison. Repeatedly.

Yet today we recognize these men as courageous examples of faith in God. The difference is that they took a stand for God, looked beyond their personal circumstances and in faith allowed the hand of God to lead them.

Christ is calling. I want to answer.

Join me today, won't you?

Open Doors

Inside or outside. That's what a door conveys.

We can choose to stand on one side or the other. We can keep things inside or outside, open the door or close it. Some doors are found in opportunities, worship, or faithfulness. Then there are emotional doors. We can be locked in or out. The doors become prison bars, trapping us in painful situations.

Death is the final door in this life. Do you dread it or look forward to what's on the other side?

This book is your opportunity to discover how the doors in your life align with the Word of God. The choice is yours: inside or outside?

Decide for Jesus today. He is the only choice worth making. Christ is calling.

I want to answer. Join me today, won't you?

Reflecting Christ

—— through the ——

Fruit
of the
Spirit

The reflection we cast. Does it reveal us or Christ?

There is a distinction between outward appearances and true substance, and it's clear in how we live out our lives as followers of Jesus.

Why would the world accept a Christian who doesn't live like Christ? That's where the Fruit of the Spirit comes into play in our lives.

How do we know the Fruit is active in our lives? We see it in the love we show to those in need.

Decide for Jesus today. He is the only choice worth making.

CALLED CAMP
—————2025—

Moses ... freeing the Egyptian slaves and parting the Red Sea!

David ... the King and the Psalmist!

Then there's Gideon, Jonah and Jeremiah!

Each of these men had to start somewhere small: Moses ran away to live in the desert. David tended sheep. Gideon, Jonah and Jeremiah just hoped to be left alone!

What has God called you to do for the kingdom? Are you willing to say yes?

Decide for Jesus today. He is the only choice worth making.

Discovering
GOD
in the
Secret
Places

The Word reveals to us that we will never have all the answers. God has set boundaries on our knowledge.

What seems right and appropriate for us, our families, and those we affect is based on feelings, circumstances, and the emotions that drive us to react rather than to reason.

We cry, "Where are you, God?" He whispers to us, "Slow down, and you will find me."

As you read this book, challenge yourself. Choose Wonder over Worry, bask in God's Season, and let the calendar of your life be written by the One who delivers us from a life of sin and shame.

Choose to trust in God, for He is the only one deserving of our eternal adoration.

It's Not All About Sitting at the Head Table

Here's what the example of Jesus teaches us: branding isn't enough. Wearing the Christian name-tag is worthless if we don't hold up in the wash.

Do we feed the hungry? Do we clothe the naked? Are we a friend to the friendless and a comfort to the brokenhearted?

Jesus washed His disciples' feet. The Master stooped to the level of a servant, and in doing so, became a greater example of service than any soloist or evangelist ever dreamed.

The cost of leadership is heavy. The price for being "on show" rests hard on our shoulders.

Here's the lesson from our Lord:

To truly stand out in the Kingdom of God, we must first spend time on our knees.

ONE. LESS. STONE.

Our heartfelt praise is a weapon against worry and the attacks of the evil one. Our active praise motivates us into obedience and empowers us to step out in strength with the joy of Jesus on our lips.

Our praise then assumes a guiding role and serves as a prophecy for our future. It places the promise we cannot see into our grasp and gives us personal motivation and encouragement to walk in sanctification.

When we develop a personal lifestyle of passionate, daily praise, the stones will no longer be required to cry out to heaven, because we will have fulfilled Christ's command.

A The Age of Uncertainty

A Call to Stand Firm

The earth is being shaken by the forces of darkness, and there's only one way to remain secure.

Our salvation comes through standing on the Rock that is Christ. Our focus must be truly on Him.

The events of this world will try to distract us from God's saving power. What we must understand is that the chaos isn't random. God is shaking the world because He loves us.

If our life is built on the eternal Word of God, we will endure the consuming fire that is washing across the world today.

www.ingramcontent.com/pod-product-compliance
Lightning Source LLC
Chambersburg PA
CBHW070014110426
42741CB00034B/1624